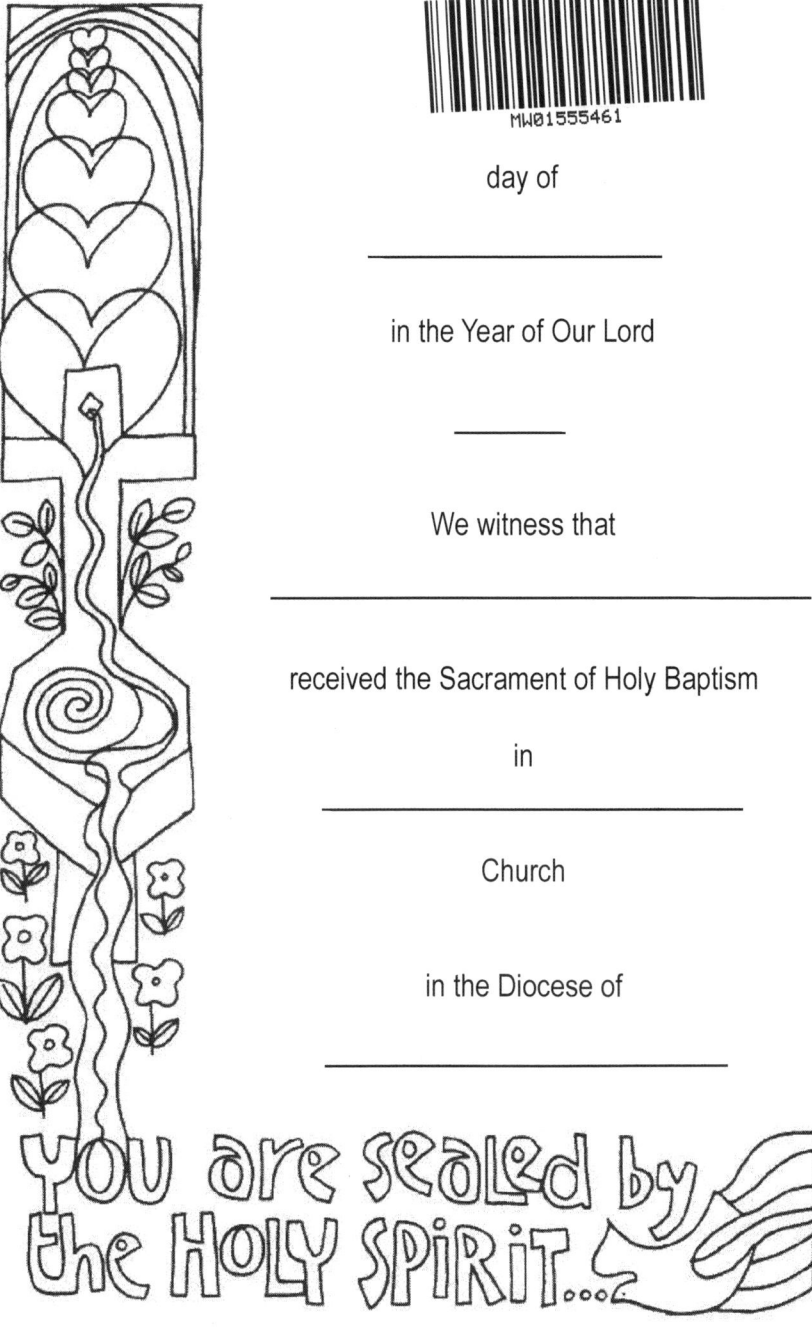

day of

_____

in the Year of Our Lord

_____

We witness that

_____

received the Sacrament of Holy Baptism

in

_____

Church

in the Diocese of

_____

You are sealed by the Holy Spirit...

_____

Presiding at the Baptism

The Parents

_____

_____

Godparents, Sponsors, Witnesses

_____

_____

_____

_____

_____

_____

_____

Introduction

This little book comes as a gift for your journey, the journey that began for you when the child first came into your lives. And now, at Baptism, the faith community joins you on the journey.

I hope that both the words and the art in this book will invite you to continue to celebrate the child, the baptism, and the abundance of God's grace through the years. I have included suggestions for the parents and the godparents; and some of the activities might appeal to grandparents. I hope you will see the suggestions as invitations — and not as "shoulds."

The blank pages in the middle of the book provide places for you to paste photos taken at the baptism, or perhaps a photo of the church in which the child was baptized. Please make it your book.

Scripture passages cited come from the New Revised Standard Version translation of the Bible. The abbreviation "BCP" indicates the Episcopal Book of Common Prayer.

Blessings on your journey.

Helen Barron
Denver Colorado

WHAT HAPPENS AT BAPTISM?

At the conclusion of the baptism, we will proclaim:

"We receive you into the household of God. Confess the faith of Christ crucified, proclaim his resurrection, and share with us in his eternal priesthood." *(Page 308, BCP)*

We will be receiving this child, this child of God. We are recognizing that this child is now a member of the body of Christ. And, we are proclaiming that we expect this child will share with us in our call to be the priesthood of all believers. We look forward to the insights this child will bring to our life together; what we will teach this child and what this child will teach us.

We will be beginning a journey together. On the journey will be the child, the parents, and the godparents. And that little circle includes siblings and other relatives, including the grandparents. That circle rests securely within the larger circle formed by the community that welcomes the child into the household of God, the body of Christ, wherever the child goes. The community that witnesses this baptism takes on — as a community — responsibilites similar to those of the parents and the godparents.

The community will promise to "do all in its power to support" this child and these parents and godparents. And so the awesome promises we make at Baptism will be sustained by the support of the entire community. And as the child "grows into the full stature of Christ," the child will be blessing the community with the gifts of this child's fresh insights and thought-provoking questions.

"We receive you into the household of God."

And in receiving this child, we are acknowledging that the child belongs already to God, has been God's for eons. We accept that God has loved this child since long before we knew the child was coming to share our world. We claim what the psalmist said:

> *"For you yourself created my inmost parts;*
> *you knit me together in my mother's womb.*
>
> *I will thank you because I am marvelously made;*
> *your works are wonderful, and I know it well.*
>
> *My body was not hidden from you,*
> *while I was being made in secret*
> *and woven in the depths of the earth."*

Psalm 139: 12-14, BCP

We receive this child.

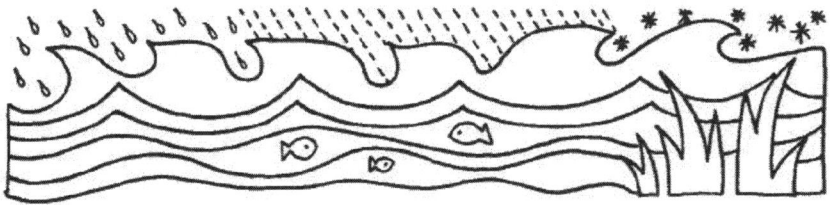

Name This Child

When the priest or bishop who presides asks you to do so, you will proclaim the name of the child. Think how much thought has already gone into what the name would be — how it would be spelled — for whom the child may be named. In the years to come, the child may choose to call himself by a nickname, or she may decide to use the initials -- or even change the name. But the name selected for the child identifies the child. We will wait in expectation for the unfolding of the gifts this child brings.

Scripture is full of "naming." Remember how God invited Adam into the process of naming the animals (Genesis 2:19)? When John the Baptist was to be born, the angel told John's father that the child was to be named John (Luke 1:13). And later in the same chapter of Luke, the angel names the baby Mary is to bear (Luke 1:31).

Naming. We will celebrate the child's name. Perhaps the name will be listed in the church bulletin the day the child is baptized. And the name will be recorded in the official records of the church.

As the child grows, the child will come to know: "this is *my* name." We will assure the child: God knows your name. God accepts you. God loves you.

Jesus heard his name called by God. Jesus also heard God say: "You are my Son, the Beloved; with you I am well pleased" (Luke 3:22b). We can assure this child that she or he is also beloved by God, that God is well pleased with this child. When we know we are loved, isn't it much easier to take the risks we find in life? When we know we will be forgiven, isn't it much less difficult to admit we have made a mistake and tell God we know we have? And doesn't knowing that God knows our name make God so much more accessible to us?

We name this child.

WHAT DO WE EXPECT DURING BAPTISM?

At baptism, the power of God the Father, God the Son, and God the Holy Spirit is present.

At baptism, we hear the Thanksgiving over the Water (pages 306 and 307 of the Book of Common Prayer): the sweep of salvation history in two succinct paragraphs-- rich paragraphs that will radiate meaning over the years. Perhaps they are like a pebble dropped in a lake. The ripples will continue on their way out of our sight right now.

During the prayer of Thanksgiving over the Water, we proclaim that we have noticed the powerful place of water in all life. Over, through, and in water we trace our salvation history. In the water of baptism, by it and through it, we come with Christ — through death, resurrection, and rebirth. Cleansed from whatever sin, this, child of God baptized, is coming into our community, in fellowship with all those who come to God in faith.

This child has new life in the Holy Spirit. With us, any time the child falls short of the mark, the child can turn around and get right with God. God waits, continually, for us to choose to come back to God.

Water is the mysterious vehicle. Why water? we could well ask. Why not something else? Water dries up so quickly. And yet, what do you think of when you think of water? Cool refreshing water to drink when we are thirsty? Deep, dark foreboding water in which we could drown? Cleansing water that washes away not only soil, but soothes our cares? Water cascading over rocks, or collecting in peaceful pools? What pictures come up on your mental screen when you hear "water?" When was it scary? Refreshing? When was it just plain fun?

What experiences of water has this child had since leaving the watery security of the womb? Was the child afraid of the first bath, or did the child take to it like a baby duck? Is the child old enough to have had wading pool fun? Stomping in mud puddles fun? We give thanks for the gift of water.

BUT FIRST:
WHAT DO WE PROMISE AT BAPTISM?

So many things we proclaim come in threes. We have three things we will "renounce": Satan, evil powers, and sinful desires, for they all turn us away from God. Then, we have three "announcements": We accept Jesus Christ as our Savior, put our whole trust in his grace and love, and promise to follow and obey Jesus as our Lord.

And who is going to help us as we live out these promises? "All who witness these vows," that's who. All will say in a strong voice: "We will." All, not just the godparents and the family assembled. All. Those you already know and those you have not even met. All vow to "do all in their power to support these persons in their life in Christ." All are here to help us.

Then, all say the creed (p. 304, Book of Common Prayer) which proclaims what we believe. Then we go on (pages 304 and 305) to answer five "will yous".

"I will, with God's help."

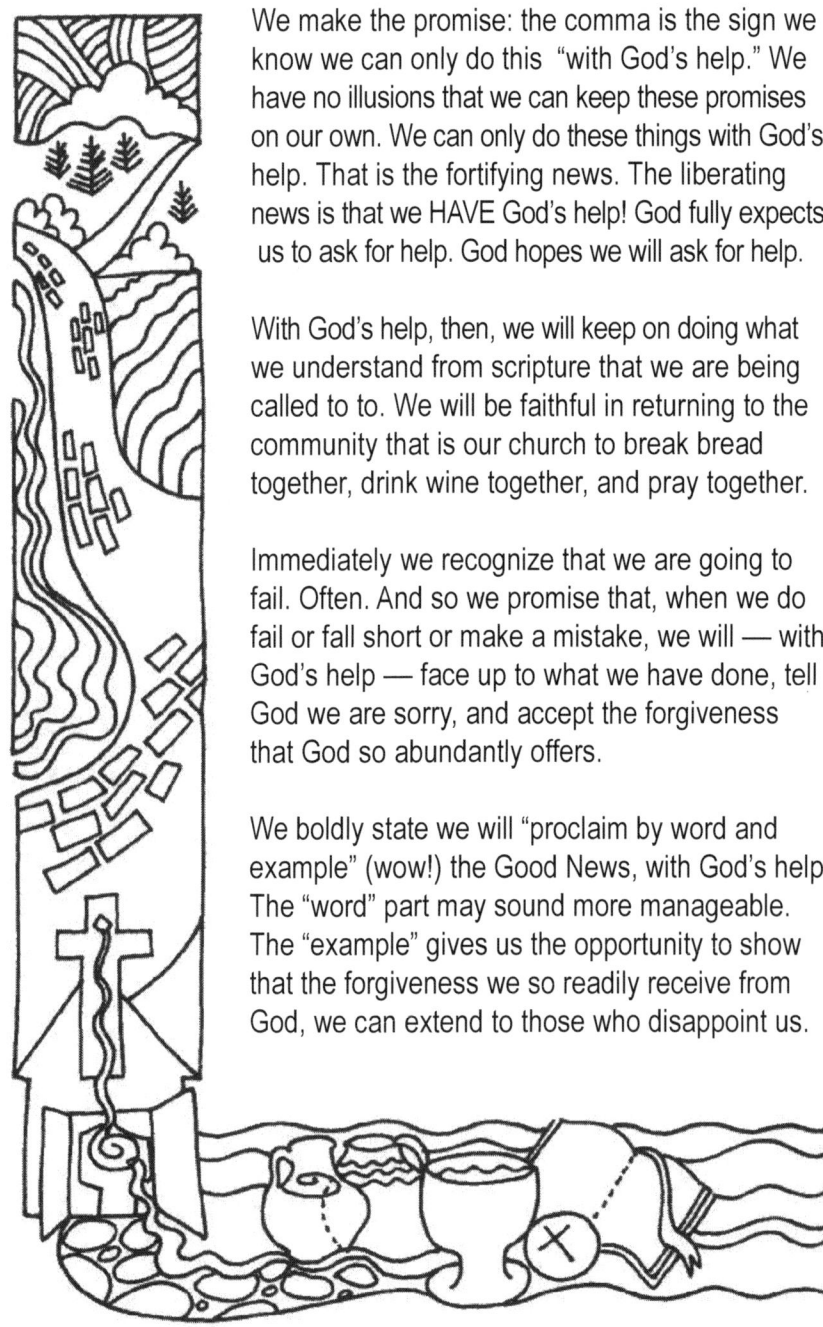

We make the promise: the comma is the sign we know we can only do this "with God's help." We have no illusions that we can keep these promises on our own. We can only do these things with God's help. That is the fortifying news. The liberating news is that we HAVE God's help! God fully expects us to ask for help. God hopes we will ask for help.

With God's help, then, we will keep on doing what we understand from scripture that we are being called to to. We will be faithful in returning to the community that is our church to break bread together, drink wine together, and pray together.

Immediately we recognize that we are going to fail. Often. And so we promise that, when we do fail or fall short or make a mistake, we will — with God's help — face up to what we have done, tell God we are sorry, and accept the forgiveness that God so abundantly offers.

We boldly state we will "proclaim by word and example" (wow!) the Good News, with God's help. The "word" part may sound more manageable. The "example" gives us the opportunity to show that the forgiveness we so readily receive from God, we can extend to those who disappoint us.

With God's help we will look for Christ's face in each person we meet. We will honor the child of God we are by loving ourselves and then, in turn, loving our neighbor with as much love as we extend ourselves.

Then we take a deep breath and proclaim that, with God's help, we will strive for justice, for peace among all people, and will respect the dignity of every human being.

"I will, with God's help."

Immediately we plunge into prayer. We have claimed that God will help us: now we offer our "I will" up to God. We trust in God, we thank God for water, we offer the child to be baptized.

Directly, we will thank God that this child has been forgiven and raised to the new life of grace. We claim this child will be sustained in the Holy Spirit. And then, this is what we ask for this child:

. . . an inquiring and discerning heart,
the courage to will and to persevere,
a spirit to know and to love you,
and the gift of joy and wonder in all your works.
Amen.

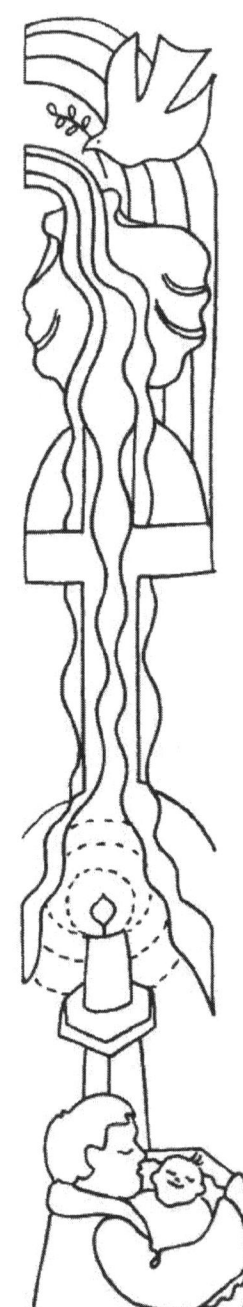

Then the sign of the cross is traced on the child's forehead. And this is what the officiant proclaims:

> . . .*you are sealed by the Holy Spirit*
> *in Baptism*
> *and marked as Christ's own forever.*
> *Amen.*

And then, all of us together, will boldly proclaim:

> *We receive you into the household of God.*
> *Confess the faith of Christ crucified,*
> *proclaim his resurrection,*
> *and share with us in his eternal priesthood.*

How can we keep the child, this special child of God, from getting obscured by the beauty of the words and the power of the event?

No matter how young the child, could the child possibly experience the water and the baptismal font at your church before the day of the baptism? Could you take the child into the church, pour some water in the font, and let the child enjoy the feel of the water? Couldn't this have the potential of making the baptism even more special to the child?

you are Christ's own forever

If there are older siblings, could they be included in the service? Could they light the candles, serve as acolytes or ushers, read a lesson or, the litany? How can they be invited to see this as an opportunity to celebrate their own baptism, which they may have been too young to remember? Could they be invited to place their hands in the water?

What if the godparents fashioned a square of cloth to be used as the "towel" at the baptism, something the child could hold for comfort and could keep to enjoy later?

Could the godparents create a special candle to be lit the first time at the baptism of the child and later on the anniversary of the baptism each year? A pillar candle, at least 2 inches wide, could be decorated with designs cut from sheets of wax. And if the child is no longer an infant, the child could collaborate in the design.

If carpentry skills are available to the godparents, perhaps they could fashion a simple wood box to hold the treasures that will accumulate during the relationship. The box could be a freshly-painted small tool box, or tackle box, or even a basket.

Can we who have witnessed the vows and made the promises, commit to a regular time to pray for this child? Perhaps the two prayers, offered at the Baptism and printed on the next page, would serve us.

(Insert the child's name -- and the appropriate pronoun.)

This our prayer for you:

*Heavenly Father, we thank you
that by water and the Holy Spirit
you have bestowed upon*

_____

*your servant,
the forgiveness of sin,
and have raised _____ to the new life of grace.
Sustain _____, O Lord, in your Holy Spirit.
Give _____ an inquiring and discerning heart,
the courage to will and to persevere,
a spirit to know and to love you,
and the gift of joy and wonder
in all your works. Amen.*

And we claim this promise:

_____

. . . you are sealed by the Holy Spirit
in Baptism
and marked as Christ's own for ever.
Amen.

PHOTOS

PHOTOS

PHOTOS

PHOTOS

How Do We
"SHARE IN THE ROYAL PRIESTHOOD OF JESUS CHRIST?"

Delighting in the infant or young child that has just been baptized, this question seems a bit overwhelming, doesn't it? Especially to sleep-deprived parents.

We have this new life in Christ, a God we can trust, and the Holy Spirit to guide us. So we will drop a few pebbles in the lake and the ripples will continue on, out of our sight right now. We can work out what this royal priesthood is becoming as we accept the grace and peace we have been promised.

Almost immediately we will notice a rhythm, a balance. Our private celebrations of the uniqueness of the child will lead us out to share with others. Our times with others will create teachable moments for us and the child. As we teach the child, we will be learning from the child.

As we worship in community, we will want to include the child, showing the child what we are doing so the child will want to participate. We can teach the child to say "Amen" with us. Very early the child can learn:

> Christ has died,
> Christ is risen.
> Christ will come again.

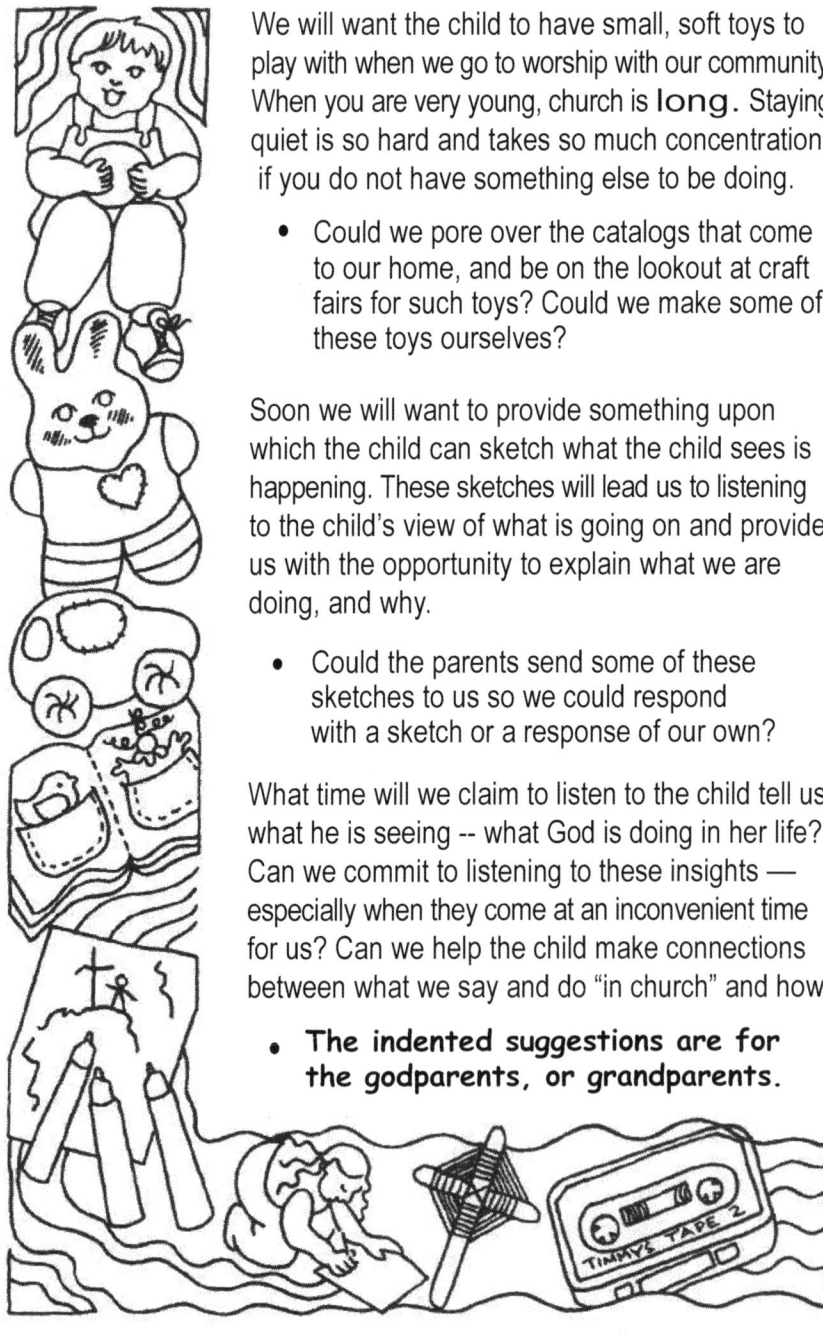

We will want the child to have small, soft toys to play with when we go to worship with our community. When you are very young, church is **long**. Staying quiet is so hard and takes so much concentration, if you do not have something else to be doing.

- Could we pore over the catalogs that come to our home, and be on the lookout at craft fairs for such toys? Could we make some of these toys ourselves?

Soon we will want to provide something upon which the child can sketch what the child sees is happening. These sketches will lead us to listening to the child's view of what is going on and provide us with the opportunity to explain what we are doing, and why.

- Could the parents send some of these sketches to us so we could respond with a sketch or a response of our own?

What time will we claim to listen to the child tell us what he is seeing -- what God is doing in her life? Can we commit to listening to these insights — especially when they come at an inconvenient time for us? Can we help the child make connections between what we say and do "in church" and how

- **The indented suggestions are for the godparents, or grandparents.**

we are choosing to live out our lives? What times in our lives together, for example, evoke spontaneous prayer? In what ordinary situations do we include a prayer the child can say along with us? (Meals may or may not work, bedtime might be the time, you will find out what is right for you.)

- Could we write notes to the child telling the child what we are praying for -- for that child? Could they include remembering: the photo of you I am looking at reminds me of . . .

We have promised to "persevere in resisting evil," and when we have missed the mark, to repent and return to the Lord. Like so many things we try to teach children, this one in particular has the effect that what we DO creates such a loud sound that it can well drown out what we say. To a large extent, the child's ability to forgive and to receive forgiveness will depend on what the child observes in the behavior of the parents and those closest to the child. Not quite what we want to hear!

- Will we be quick to own our actions when we have failed the child? What do you think happens to a child's spirit when we tell the child we are sorry and we ask for the child's forgiveness?

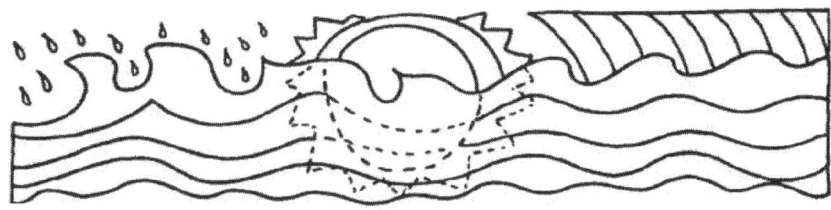

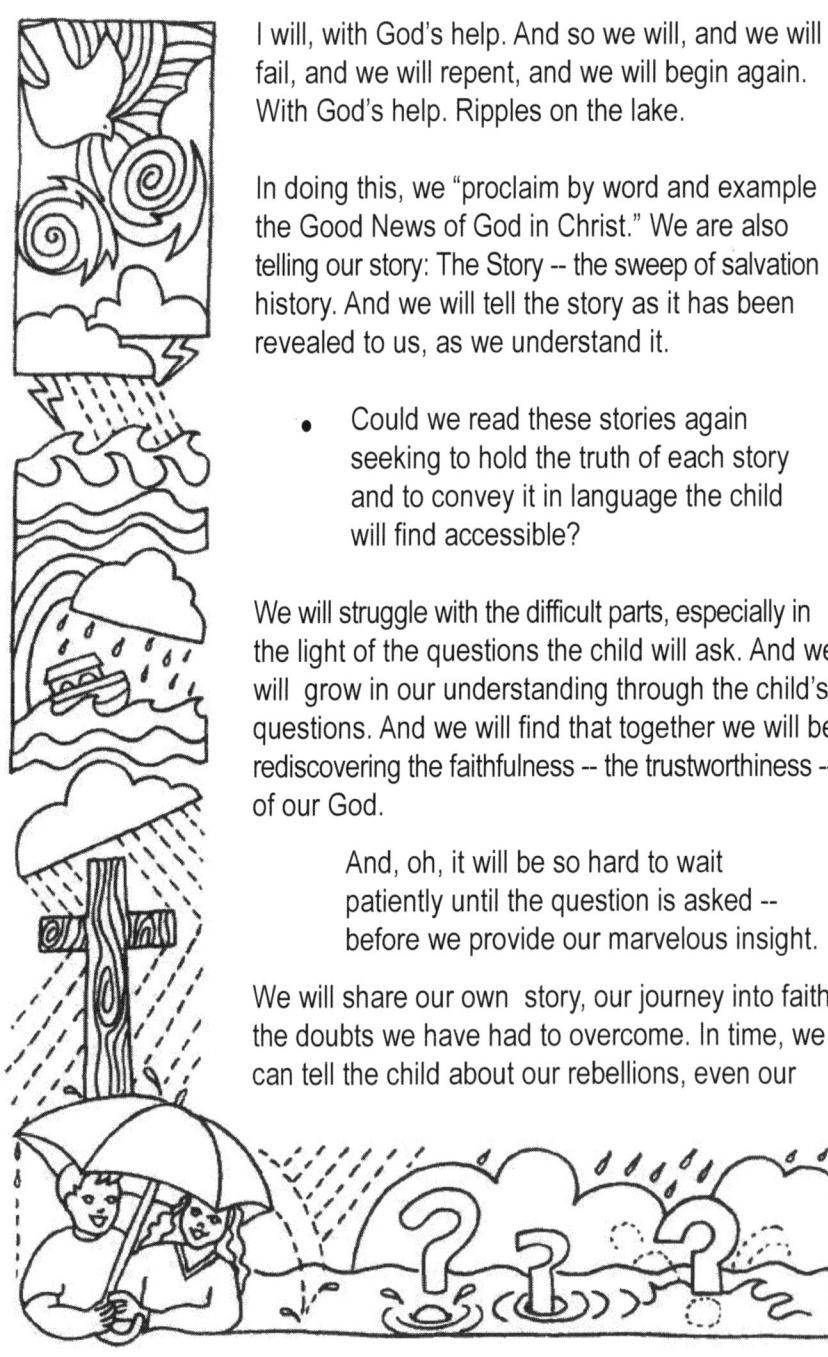

I will, with God's help. And so we will, and we will fail, and we will repent, and we will begin again. With God's help. Ripples on the lake.

In doing this, we "proclaim by word and example the Good News of God in Christ." We are also telling our story: The Story -- the sweep of salvation history. And we will tell the story as it has been revealed to us, as we understand it.

- Could we read these stories again seeking to hold the truth of each story and to convey it in language the child will find accessible?

We will struggle with the difficult parts, especially in the light of the questions the child will ask. And we will grow in our understanding through the child's questions. And we will find that together we will be rediscovering the faithfulness -- the trustworthiness -- of our God.

> And, oh, it will be so hard to wait patiently until the question is asked -- before we provide our marvelous insight.

We will share our own story, our journey into faith, the doubts we have had to overcome. In time, we can tell the child about our rebellions, even our rejection of the story -- if we have experienced that. And we will be containers for what the child brings us of her journey and we will hold for the child the insights he has brought us. We will assure the child that the child's experience enriches our own. We will receive the child's story along with the child.

- Could we get in the habit of noticing what calls out to be kept: beginning with the bulletin from the Baptism and adding photos and the art work the child provides as well as special sticks we find together and some of the "beautiful" rocks we will discover?

How will we "seek and serve Christ in all persons"? Will the child be able to observe our seeing Christ in each member of the family? In the people we come in contact with, in traffic, at the supermarket, on the playground? And what will our reaction be to people who appear to be quite different from us -- in skin color, economic condition, speech, education, nationality?

- What behaviors will the child see in us when the child is in our company?

Will the child see in us a "scarcity" mentality: guarding things for our own needs? Or, will the child see in us an attitude of "abundance": God has richly given to us and

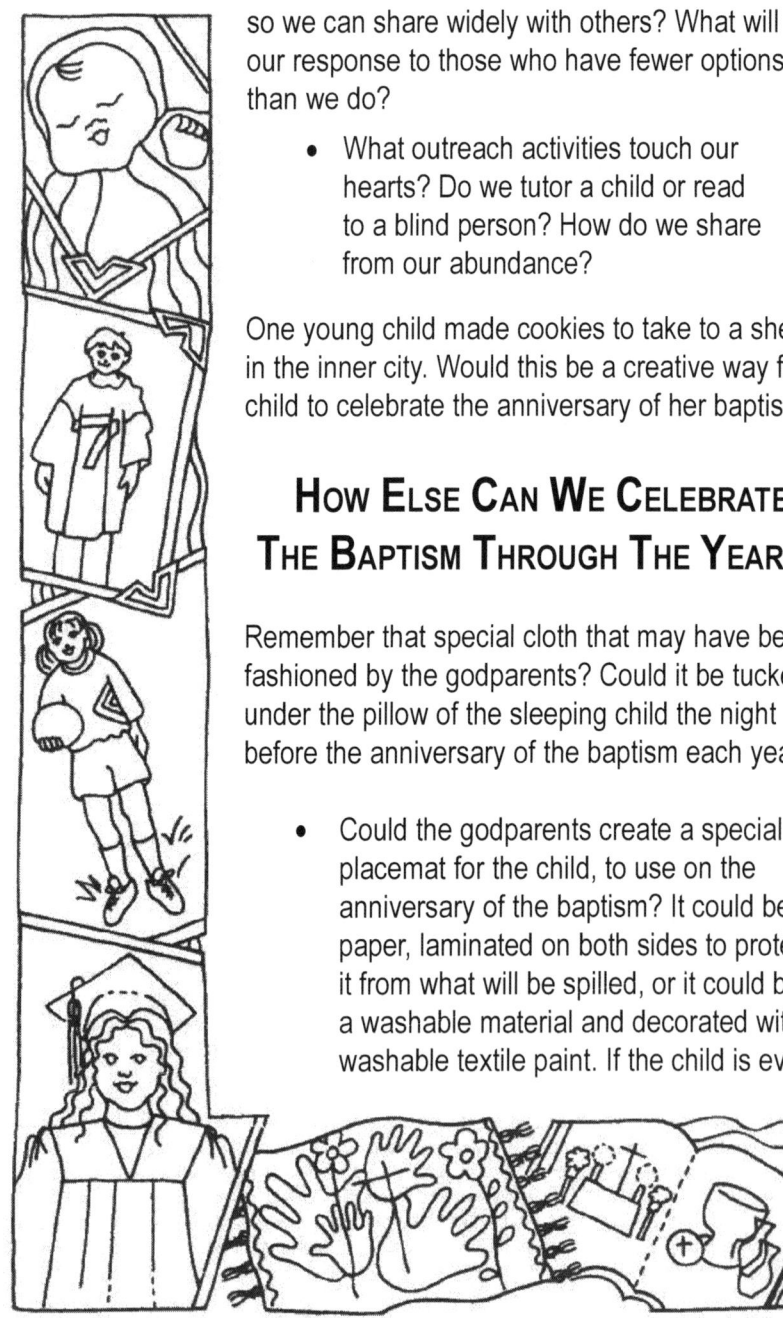

so we can share widely with others? What will be our response to those who have fewer options than we do?

- What outreach activities touch our hearts? Do we tutor a child or read to a blind person? How do we share from our abundance?

One young child made cookies to take to a shelter in the inner city. Would this be a creative way for a child to celebrate the anniversary of her baptism?

How Else Can We Celebrate The Baptism Through The Years?

Remember that special cloth that may have been fashioned by the godparents? Could it be tucked under the pillow of the sleeping child the night before the anniversary of the baptism each year?

- Could the godparents create a special placemat for the child, to use on the anniversary of the baptism? It could be paper, laminated on both sides to protect it from what will be spilled, or it could be a washable material and decorated with washable textile paint. If the child is even a few months old, the child could collaborate in the design.

Could you and the child make a prayer book for the child to take along to church? Perhaps it could have space for a drawing the child makes of what the altar looks like, or the chalice, the bread, the candles. It could include the prayers the child is learning (the Lord's Prayer and some of the responses the congregation makes). It could include the child's drawing of Bible stories you and the child have discovered together. It might even include drawings or photos of people the child chooses to pray for as well as blank pages to accommodate insights the child gets during the worship service.

Could you make a quilt together, or individual squares to be sewn together as a quilt? The squares could mark special times in the child's life: yes, the date of the baptism, but also the date the first tooth came out, the date of the first solo flight on the bicycle, whatever.

- Could we provide squares marking things we did together: the fishing trip we took, or the garden we planted together?

Could we get in the habit of scouting for "good news"? We may complain about the violence in the media, yet rarely a day goes by without some story of human courage, tenacity, generosity, care, and just plain good fun. Could

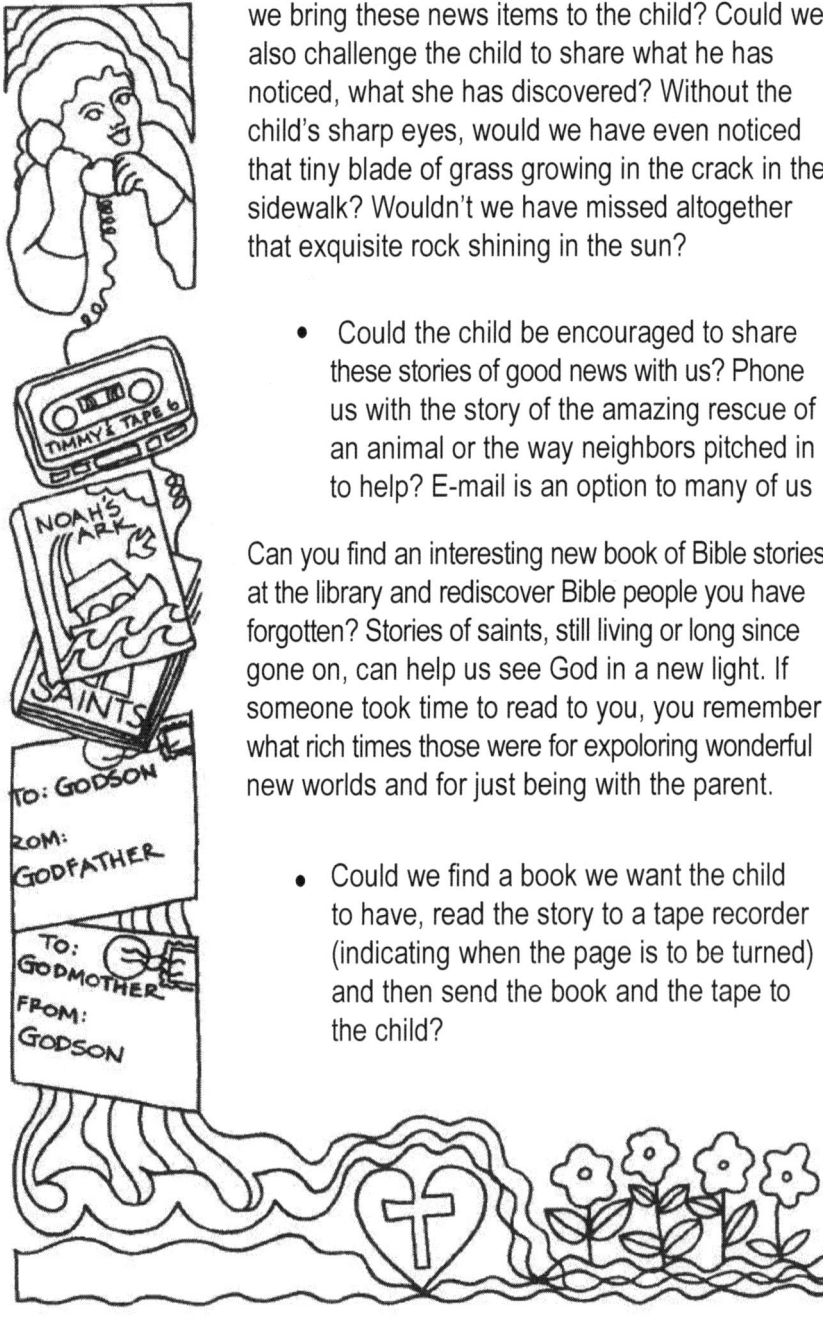

we bring these news items to the child? Could we also challenge the child to share what he has noticed, what she has discovered? Without the child's sharp eyes, would we have even noticed that tiny blade of grass growing in the crack in the sidewalk? Wouldn't we have missed altogether that exquisite rock shining in the sun?

- Could the child be encouraged to share these stories of good news with us? Phone us with the story of the amazing rescue of an animal or the way neighbors pitched in to help? E-mail is an option to many of us

Can you find an interesting new book of Bible stories at the library and rediscover Bible people you have forgotten? Stories of saints, still living or long since gone on, can help us see God in a new light. If someone took time to read to you, you remember what rich times those were for expoloring wonderful new worlds and for just being with the parent.

- Could we find a book we want the child to have, read the story to a tape recorder (indicating when the page is to be turned) and then send the book and the tape to the child?

When the child is in grade school and enjoying making up stories, could you begin a story -- perhaps about some imaginary people -- and then dispatch the story?

- We could add a few paragraphs, taking the story to an suspenseful place and then send the story back for the child to add the next potential twist.

The rhythm continues, in to listen, out to respond. And we continue to see the ripples on the lake.

AND HOW WILL WE DO AT LETTING GO?

Unless the child takes some journey, asks some questions, jettisons some baggage, the journey will never be the child's own journey and the faith will never be the child's owned faith. If we are fortunate, the child will take this adventure when he is still under his parents' roof, while parents are still responsible for her shelter; while communication -- however tenuous -- is still going on.

What is this journey the child must take? When the child is very young, the child looks to the parents for cues: what is going on here? The child prays the prayers the parent teaches and does the activities the teacher selects.

The fortunate child is invited to offer his observations, share what she has noticed. The outside dimensions of the faith are largely set by the parents and their community. And most of the child's questions, however unanswerable they may seem, (What does God look like?") can be met with responses that encourage the child to continue to explore.

By early grade school the child is thinking more concretely, noticing whether things are "fair or unfair," and is often unsatisfied with the responses we offer. (How do we answer the child's plea: "Why don't we just *feed* all the hungry children?") Can we make space for the child's doubts, so these doubts do not have to stay inside the child and fester? Can we admit to not having all the answers and at the same time express with our words and lives that we find God to be trustworthy?

Will the child continue to know our love to be an unconditional love, and not a love dependent upon meeting our expectations? We pray for grace to love unconditionally.

Somewhere, perhaps as early as grade school or as late a high school, the child must go inward for a journey that takes the child from the faith of the

you are sealed by the Holy Spirit...

parents and the community to a faith the young person can own. The child will need to find a faith sufficiently large to allow for growth and one that provides the "courage to will and to persevere."

Here we will best serve this young person with "I" statements: "I have found this to be so, or it is my experience that this is true." If we are comfortable asking: "What do you think?" we must be sure we have a place to accept the answer, especially if we do not agree.

In God's mysterious plan, some of these children will grow up, choose the faith that nurtures us, slide right in beside us in the pews and worship along with us. Thanks be to God. Some will wander into expressions of faith that startle or appall us, or may even appear to us to be jettisoning the whole faith journey. Whatever the journey they take, we can stand in front of a photo of this young person, daily, and reclaim again the promise made at their baptism:

You are sealed by the Holy Spirit in Baptism
and marked as Christ's own for ever.
Amen.

Prayer Suggestions, all from The Book of Common Prayer

Lord, God, almighty and everlasting Father, you have brought us in safety to this new day: Preserve us with your mighty power, that we may not fall into sin, nor be overcome by adversity; and in all we do, direct us to the fulfilling of your purpose; through Jesus Christ our Lord, Amen.

Page 100

May the God of hope fill us with all joy and peace in believing through the power of the Holy Spirit. Amen.

Page 102

(This prayer from Compline makes a gentle lullaby):

Guide us waking, O Lord, and guard us sleeping; that awake we may watch with Christ, and asleep we may rest in peace.   *Page 134*

Almighty God, by our baptism into the death and resurrection of your Son Jesus Christ, you turn us from the old life of sin: Grant that we, being reborn to new life in him, may live in righteousness and holiness all our days; through Jesus Christ our Lord, who lives and reigns with you and the Holy Spirit, one God, now and for ever. Amen.

Page 254

Almighty God, heavenly Father, you have blessed us with the joy and care of children: Give us calm strength and patient wisdom as we bring them up, that we may teach them to love whatever is just and true and good, following the example of our Savior Jesus Christ. Amen.

Page 829

The 23rd Psalm

The LORD is my shepherd;
  I shall not be in want.

He makes me lie down in green pastures
  and leads me beside still waters.

He revives my soul
  and guides me along right pathways for his Name's sake.

Though I walk through the valley of the shadow of death,
  I shall fear no evil;
for you are with me;
  your rod and your staff, they comfort me.

You spread a table before me in the presence of those
    who trouble me;
  you have anointed my head with oil,
    and my cup is running over.

Surely your goodness and mercy shall follow me all the
    days of my life,
  and I will dwell in the house of the LORD for ever.

Page 613

(For a birthday - Substitute "her" if the child is a girl)

Watch over thy child, O Lord, as his days increase; bless and guide him wherever he may be. Strengthen him when he stands; comfort him when discouraged or sorrowful; raise him up if he fall; and in his heart may thy peace which passeth understanding abide all the days of his life; through Jesus Christ our Lord, Amen.

Page 830

Art by: Victoria Bergesen

Written by: Helen Barron

Creative Input: Anne Thulson
　　　　　　　　The Rev. Sally Brown

Edited by: Jo Youngquist

Quotations from the Book of Common Prayer, published by Church Hymnal Corporation, used with permission.

Scripture references: The New Revised Standard Version Bible published by the Division of Christian Education of the National Council of the Churches of Christ in the United States of America.

© 1997, 2002, 2011, Helen Barron. All Rights Reserved.

ISBN 978-1-59518-052-0

Published by:

CANDLE PRESS

www.candlepress.com
303 • 337 • 6852
e-mail: candlepress.com

Made in the USA
San Bernardino, CA
04 April 2014